ARCHITECTURE TOURS L.A. GUIDEBOOK
HANCOCK PARK / MIRACLE MILE

ARCHITECTURE TOURS L.A. GUIDEBOOK
HANCOCK PARK / MIRACLE MILE

LAURA MASSINO SMITH

Schiffer Publishing Ltd

4880 Lower Valley Road, Atglen, PA 19310 USA

Library of Congress Cataloging-in-Publication Data

Smith, Laura Massino.
   Architecture tours, L.A. guidebook : Hancock Park-Miracle Mile / Laura Massino Smith.
      p. cm.
   ISBN 0-7643-2297-4 (pbk.)
I. Architecture—California—Los Angeles—Tours. 2. Automobile travel—California—Los Angeles—Tours. 3. Los Angeles (Calif.)—Buildings, structures, etc.—Tours. I. Title: Hancock Park-Miracle Mile. II. Title.

NA735.L55S5518 2005
720'.9794'94—dc22

2005008133

Designed by Mark David Bowyer
Type set in Futura BdCn BT / Lydian BT & Humanist521 Lt BT

ISBN: 0-7643-2297-4
Printed in China

DEDICATION

To my extraordinary husband, Drew, whose undying love, patience, encouragement, and support have guided me to discover my true passion.

Published by Schiffer Publishing Ltd.
4880 Lower Valley Road
Atglen, PA 19310
Phone: (610) 593-1777; Fax: (610) 593-2002
E-mail: Info@schifferbooks.com

For the largest selection of fine reference books on this and related subjects, please visit our web site at www.schifferbooks.com
We are always looking for people to write books on new and related subjects. If you have an idea for a book please contact us at the above address.

This book may be purchased from the publisher.
Include $3.95 for shipping.
Please try your bookstore first.
You may write for a free catalog.

In Europe, Schiffer books are distributed by
Bushwood Books
6 Marksbury Ave.
Kew Gardens
Surrey TW9 4JF England
Phone: 44 (0) 20 8392-8585; Fax: 44 (0) 20 8392-9876
E-mail: info@bushwoodbooks.co.uk
Free postage in the U.K., Europe; air mail at cost.

ARCHITECTURE TOURS L.A.

www.architecturetoursla.com
323.464.7868

Architecture Tours L.A. specializes in guided driving tours led by an architectural historian in a 1962 vintage Cadillac. Our tours focus on the historic and significant contemporary architecture in Los Angeles, highlighting the cultural aspects of the history of the city's built environment. This guidebook will allow you to drive yourself and discover L.A. in your own car, at your own pace. In addition to HANCOCK PARK/MIRACLE MILE, other tours offered by Architecture Tours L.A. include:

DOWNTOWN
HOLLYWOOD
WEST HOLLYWOOD/BEVERLY HILLS
SILVER LAKE
PASADENA
FRANK GEHRY

Disclaimer

It is not advisable for anyone operating a motor vehicle to read this book. Please pull your car into a safe, designated parking area before attempting any fine print. Better yet, take this tour with a friend who can act as navigator and narrator. Naturally, the best way to see it all is riding shotgun with the author! Neither the author nor the publisher assumes responsibility for moving violations committed while intoxicated by this tour.

NOTE TO TOUR GOERS

The sites included in this self-guided tour represent the architectural highlights of HANCOCK PARK/MIRACLE MILE. This tour is meant to be an overview, a starting point of sorts, and is intended to give the participant a feeling for the neighborhood. By no means does the tour include everything of interest. Numerous books of ponderous proportions have been written to that end, and if your interest is piqued, you might refer to the bibliography in the back of this book for further reading.

Herein, within a matter of hours you will glean a pretty good understanding of what historically happened, and what is currently happening architecturally in HANCOCK PARK/MIRACLE MILE. The photographs herein are for quick identification of what you will be seeing up close, in full scale. Many of the commercial buildings in this area are accessible to the public and can be seen from inside. The criteria for inclusion are the historical, cultural, and architectural significance of a site and the fact that it can be seen easily (relatively) from the street. So relax and have a great ride!

INTRODUCTION

Hancock Park and Miracle Mile are adjacent areas within the city of Los Angeles that represent many diverse neighborhoods and architectural styles. From the Post-Modern "chicken shack" starting point in Koreatown, to the grand homes and apartment buildings of Windsor Square and Hancock Park, to the Art Deco, English Tudor, French Chateauesque, and Spanish Colonial Revival style retail establishments, offices, and theaters of the Miracle Mile, almost every architectural style is present in these areas.

Many affluent residents of Hancock Park and Windsor Square have chosen to live in historic homes built during the 1920s in the English Tudor Revival and Spanish Mediterranean styles, although the area does contain a large single-family home designed in the Art Deco style – a true rarity. Another home, designed in the 1920s for the architect himself in the French Chateauesque/Farmhouse style, is located here, as is a contemporary architect's home composed of corrugated steel and glass geometric forms. You'll also find more modest homes built during the beginning of the 20th century in the Craftsman and Victorian styles, and one built in the late 1890s in the Shingle Style and moved to Hancock Park. Apartments in the Spanish Colonial Revival style, French Chateauesque, and early and late Art Deco styles, as well as theaters from the same time period exist here. The work of one of the most important architects in Los Angeles from the 1920s to the 1950s, Rudolf M. Schindler, is here in the form of two International Style, or Mid-Century Modern, apartment complexes.

The history of the area's formation is one of Los Angeles' expansion westward. From the churches, originally located Downtown in the historic core of Los Angeles, needing more room and moving to the eastern end of Wilshire Boulevard, to the creation in the 1920s of the Miracle Mile, a "new" commercial and retail district a few miles west of Downtown. The Miracle Mile had elegant and sophisticated department stores, which were some of the first to have parking lots – a new concept in the 1920s and an indication of the automobile's influence in the formation of the city. Wealth from oil helped to create Hancock Park, but the original park, where the Hancock family home was located, is now the site of the Los Angeles County Museum of Art, as well as the other museums of "Museum Row," and the La Brea Tar Pits. Fossils continue to be dug up from the tar pit site.

Many of the buildings in the Miracle Mile have undergone extensive restorations and some are being used for purposes other than what they were originally designed for. Bullock's Wilshire Department Store, once the most elegant department store in the city, was rescued by Southwestern Law School in the 1990s and is now being used as the school's library. The Wiltern Theater had fallen into disrepair, but was restored in the mid-1980s. The Chapman Market and Studio was also restored in the late 1980s. More recently, the American Cement Corporation Building from the early 1960s has been restored and is now residential loft space. The fate of the 1920s Ambassador Hotel, where American royalty such as the Vanderbilts and Duponts wintered and where Robert F. Kennedy was assassinated in 1968, currently hangs in the balance. A school will be built there, but it remains to be seen if any preservation of the existing structure will occur.

Changing and growing population and demographics are shaping the area in the form of Korean shops, churches, and businesses. The stretch of Wilshire Boulevard near the Ambassador Hotel was terribly run down in the early 1990s, and after the riots of 1992 and the earthquake of 1994, the area now shows signs of major improvement and revitalization. Young professionals are moving into older apartment buildings in the neighborhoods behind the Miracle Mile and eastern Wilshire Boulevard, and the parks once thought of as dangerous are starting to get cleaned up.

The mansions of Hancock Park and Windsor Square remain as they always have and an HPOZ (Historic Preservation Overlay Zone) in Windsor Square, which was the source of a strong controversy, looks as though it will be instated to help assure and preserve the integrity of a very historic area.

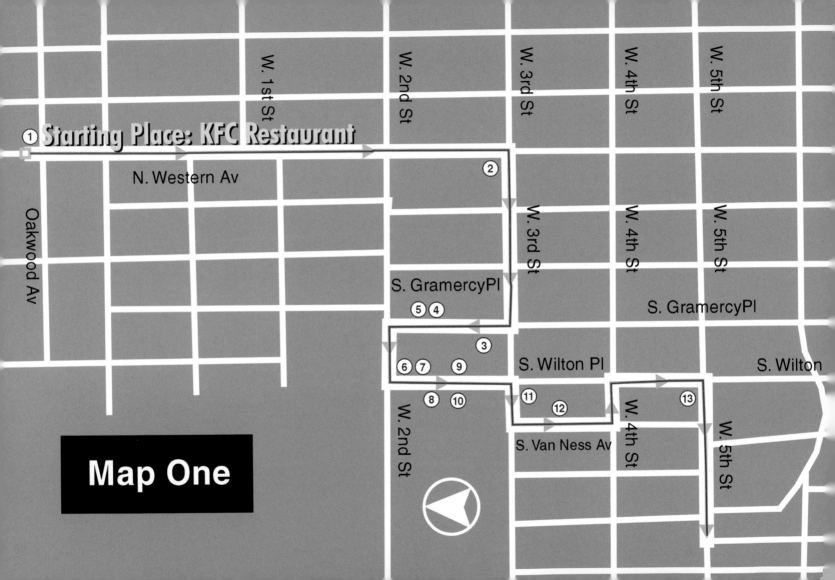

Map One

340 North Western Avenue (cross street Oakwood Avenue)

1) This building was designed in 1991 by the architectural firm of Grinstein/Daniels (Elyse Grinstein and Jeff Daniels) and is a good example of Deconstructivist Post-Modern architecture. Historically, this architectural style directly followed Modernism. The concept of "deconstructing" a building is the metaphor here. It looks as though parts of the building have been removed. Notice the use of industrial materials, such as the corrugated metal walls in back, and the exposed ductwork. The use of this type of material shows a willingness to expose the inner workings of the building and elevate the materials to a level of beauty. The fragmentation of the whole indicates a metaphorical deconstruction of the building. Notice how the shape of the structure with the curved wall in front alludes to the shape of a bucket (of chicken), creating a partial bucket form. The metal fins on the curved wall give it a sense of movement and the block form on top has the KFC logo.

The owner of this particular franchise is an art collector and friend of the architect. He asked the architects if they would ever consider designing a

1) **Kentucky Fried Chicken Restaurant, 1991, Grinstein/Daniels, 340 NORTH WESTERN AVE.**

"chicken shack." They eagerly agreed to the challenge. They were given an enormous amount of creative freedom because the owner had an appreciation for the arts and owned a few of the restaurants, which gave him more clout with the company. The owner was also an engineer and was so interested in the construction process that he built a steel scale model of the structure. The gritty neighborhood called for gritty materials, so the industrial materials left exposed seem to fit right in. This is one of the few two-story KFC restaurants in the city, and a dumb waiter inside is used to deliver orders to the second floor. This is also probably the most distinctive KFC restaurant in the city.

You are now in the area of Los Angeles known as Koreatown. You will notice that the signage is written mostly in Korean. There was a massive migration in the 1960s and '70s, and subsequently, Los Angeles has the largest Korean population outside of Korea. Koreatown is quite a large area and is still growing. There are self-sufficient businesses of all sorts, churches, schools, medical facilities, restaurants, and residences. Most of the buildings now occupied by Korean businesses and organizations are in existing buildings from the earlier part of the 20th century. There are very few examples of the traditional Korean architectural style, although it can be seen in some restaurant facades and some newer buildings. This is an indication of the younger Korean community's desire to be Americanized and assimilate into American culture.

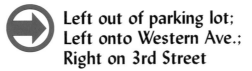

Left out of parking lot; Left onto Western Ave.; Right on 3rd Street

2) The black and gold building here on the right-hand corner of 3rd Street is an excellent example of Art Deco architecture. Art Deco takes its name from an exhibition in the early 1920s in Paris called "The Exposition of Industrial and Decorative Arts." The Art Deco style was popular in the 1920s and 1930s. Black glazed terra cotta tiles unify the structure, and the gold decoration at the top conveys a feeling of luxury. Created as a clothing store in 1931, the Selig Building, as it was originally called (a.k.a. Crocker Bank Building), was designed by architect Arthur E. Harvey. Now it is home to a variety of shops. You will see the Wilshire Professional Building, another of Arthur Harvey's buildings, later on this tour. He also designed the Chateau Elysee Hotel on Franklin Avenue in Hollywood, which is now the Scientology Celebrity Center and can be seen on the HOLLYWOOD tour. This building is listed as Historic-Cultural Monument #298 by the City of Los Angeles.

2) Selig Building, (a.k.a. Crocker Bank Building; now various shops), 1931, Arthur E. Harvey , 4357 3RD STREET (273 WESTERN AVE.)

Right on Gramercy Place

3) The house here on your left with the wonderful stone chimney is the Schlegal House, built circa 1915 by the Schlegal Brothers, who were contractors. It was designed in a version of the Craftsman style with shingles, exposed rafter tails, and a beautiful river rock stone chimney as a focal point of the exterior.

3) Schlegal House, c. 1915, Schlegel Bros. (owner/contractor), 249 SOUTH GRAMERCY PLACE

4) There are many Arts and Crafts, or Craftsman style homes on this street, but the Isenstein House, here on your right, is an excellent example of the Spanish Mission style. This style was fashioned after the Spanish Missions of California and the Southwest, which were built in the late 1700s in the name of Spain. When Wilshire Boulevard started to develop into a commercial street, many structures were moved from there, and this was one of them. The home was formerly a church and that's why it looks as though there has been some remodeling, but the Spanish Mission style remains. The house is characterized by a flat facade with a central arch and deeply recessed stucco walls made to look like adobe.

4) Isenstein House, c. 1912, J. Isenstein (owner/contractor), 222 SOUTH GRAMERCY PLACE

5) The Craftsman house with the tapered stone pillars, here on your right, was built circa 1915. No original building permit record could be found so the architect's name remains a mystery. In the late 19th and early 20th centuries pattern books could be purchased and a homeowner and contractor could build without the aid of an architect. Houses could also be ordered from companies such as Sears Roebuck and the parts would be numbered and shipped as a kit to be put together by the homeowner. This house was designed in the more typical Craftsman style with a low-pitched roof, leaded glass windows, wrap-around porch, stone columns, and wide wood front door.

The Arts and Crafts, or Craftsman style, came about as a response to the Victorian style, which directly preceded it. It was a reaction to the insensitivity of machine-made goods and sought to return to the principles of hand craftsmanship. No more fussy jigsawed decoration on the exteriors or turned-wood spindles on the front porches, as was customary in Victorian architecture. It was a return to simplicity in domestic architecture and the typical Craftsman bungalow was usually just one story. Larger versions were also designed, however, and included one-and-a-half and two-story houses. The Arts and Crafts style originated in England and proliferated throughout America, but here there was a California version. This is best seen in the work of architects Greene

& Greene in Pasadena and the well-known Gamble House, all of which can be seen on the PASADENA tour, but there are very good examples here, too.

The characteristics of Craftsman architecture featured the extensive use of wood on both the interiors and exteriors. Exposed rafter tails under the over-hanging roof, often with the corners rounded, were also typical, as were broad porches. The interior wood paneling was frequently created from oak, or golden oak, and produced a warming effect. Wood joinery was often left exposed and glorified the beauty of the wood. Wood shingles were also used extensively, as well as leaded Art Glass and decorative tile work. The fireplace was a major focal point of the home and often featured an inglenook. Materials were left as natural as possible and the houses were designed to fit into their sites with nature as unobtrusively as possible.

Influences for the Craftsman style included Japanese architectural elements, Swiss chalets, and hunting lodges. All styles that made a deeper connection with nature.

5) Craftsman House, c. 1915, (architect unknown), 218 SOUTH GRAMERCY

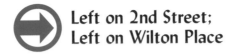

Left on 2nd Street; Left on Wilton Place

6) Here on the left corner of Wilton Place and 2nd Street is the Woolmer House, built circa 1927. City records indicate that the garage addition was built by the homeowner, but no record was found listing the original architect's name. The two-and-a-half story house's color scheme and clapboard siding are reminiscent of Victorian architecture, but it was not built during the Victorian era and is not really a true Victorian style house. At the time the house was built, a transitional style combining various aspects of more than one pure style was emerging and this fits better into that category and time period.

This section of Wilton Place is in a designated Historic Preservation Overlay Zone (HPOZ), which means that if a homeowner wants to alter the exterior of their home they must have the approval of a design review board. It is a way of preserving the architectural integrity of a neighborhood. Wilton Place has an excellent and well-preserved collection of homes built in the early years of the 20th century. This location is also listed on the National Register of Historic Places.

6) Woolmer House, c. 1927, Harry E. Woolmer (owner/contractor), WILTON PLACE AND 2ND STREET

7) Lewis S. Stone House, c. 1920, (possibly owner/contractor), 212 SOUTH WILTON PLACE

8) Churchill House, 1909, F. Pierpont Davis, 215 SOUTH WILTON PLACE

9) Craftsman/Victorian House, c. 1914, (architect unknown), 220 SOUTH WILTON PLACE

7) Next, on your left is the impressive Lewis S. Stone House with four large fluted columns in front crowned with Corinthian capitals. The house was built before 1920, most likely by the owner, as his name is the only one on the building records. Combining Neo-Classical, Victorian, and Craftsman styles, it is a well-balanced composition and makes quite a striking impression.

8) Across the street, the brown house on your right at 215 South Wilton Place is the Churchill House, designed in 1909 by F. Pierpont Davis. The house has a very straightforward design with a subdued, pared-down style. There are Craftsman-style exposed rafter tails, but they are barely visible and are almost turned under the roof. The beauty of this house lies in the simplicity of its design. This house is listed as Historic-Cultural Monument #568 by the City of Los Angeles.

9) The Craftsman/Victorian style house on the left side of the street at 220 South Wilton Place was built before 1914 because the only construction permit found was for plumbing installation. No owner or architect was listed, and it is likely that this house was built from a pattern book. This house has more characteristics of the Victorian and English styles than the Craftsman style. There are multiple rooflines, diamond pane windows, half-timber decoration, and dentil molding. Where exposed rafter tails would have been the ends have been capped. On the right side is a bay-type window below a conical shaped roof. These are all much closer to Victorian architectural styles. The Craftsman elements here are reflected in the wood frames around the windows and the low massing of the house.

10) Hayes House, c. 1919, (architect unknown), 221 SOUTH WILTON PLACE

10) The Hayes House, the brown Craftsman house on the right at 221 South Wilton Place, was built before 1919, as the earliest permit found with that date was for the addition of a porch and carport. The house is very similar to the one just seen and may have been built by the same builders.

➡ **Right on 3rd Street; Left on Van Ness Avenue**

11) You are now in the neighborhood called "Windsor Square." This is St. Brendan's Catholic church, here on the left corner of Van Ness Avenue and 3rd Street. It was built in 1927 by Emmett Martin, a second generation of the well-known Albert C. Martin family of architects, prominent in Los Angeles and still in existence. Emmett Martin was educated in France after serving in World War I. The style of the church is French Gothic with its pointed arches and steep walls and roof aspiring toward heaven. The stained glass windows were made in Germany and shipped here. All of these design characteristics, including the three-door front entrance, are typical features of French Gothic architecture, which originated in 1150 A.D. and continued to 1500 A.D.

11) St. Brendan's Church, 1927, Emmett Martin, 300 SOUTH VAN NESS AVE.

15

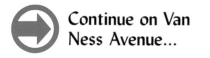
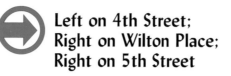
12) The Sedana House, here on your left, is a very well maintained two-story Craftsman style home. It was built in 1914, but the architect is unknown. This house embodies the characteristics of Craftsman architecture, including the extensive use of wood, copious shingling, exposed rafter tails, a low pitched roof, and wide wood door.

12) Sedana House, 1914, (architect unknown), 326 SOUTH VAN NESS AVE.

13) The Chateau Laurier apartment building, here on the corner to your right, was designed in the French 16th century Renaissance Chateauesque style. It was built in 1928 and designed by Leland A. Bryant, who was known for his Chateauesque-style apartment designs. He also designed the Trianon Apartments, seen on the HOLLYWOOD tour, and the magnificent Art Deco Sunset Towers, now the Argyle Hotel on Sunset Boulevard in West Hollywood and seen on the WEST HOLLYWOOD/BEVERLY HILLS tour. This revival style was popular in the 1920s because of America's exposure to French architecture during World War I. People were enamored with this style and brought it back home. The growing movie industry also helped to fuel this fantasy style.

13) Chateau Laurier, 1928, Leland A. Bryant, 4353-4357 5TH STREET

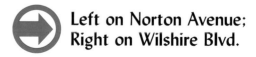

Map Two

W. 4th St (29)

W. 4th St

W. 5th St

(28)

W. 5th St (27)

Lorraine Blvd

S Irving Blvd

S. Norton Av

W. 6th St

W. 6th St

(26)

(16)

S. Bronson Av

(24) (25)

(22) (20)

Wilshire Blvd

(18) (17)

(15) (14)

Wilshire Blv

(23)

S. Lucerne Bl

(21)

S. Plymouth B

S. Windsor Blvd

(19)

Lorraine Blvd

Crenshaw Blvd

S. Bronson Av

S. Norton Av

S. Lucerne Blvd

14) Here on your right, at the corner of Norton Avenue and Wilshire Boulevard, is the site of Perino's Restaurant. The original building, dating from 1949, was remodeled by architect Paul Revere Williams in 1963 in the Regency Style for Perino's Restaurant. The original restaurant opened during the Depression in another location further east on Wilshire Boulevard. Through the fifties and sixties, when the restaurant had relocated here, it was considered to be one of L.A.'s most popular. Celebrities including Frank Sinatra, Cole Porter, Elizabeth Taylor, and Cary Grant frequented the restaurant. The restaurant was sold in 1969 and remained opened until it finally closed in 1986. Paul Williams also designed the home of restaurant owner Alex Perino and many other celebrities' homes as well. At the time of this writing, this site is to be developed into multi-unit dwellings.

Paul Williams was born in Los Angeles in 1894 and attended the Los Angeles School of Art and the Atelier of Beaux Arts Institute of Design in Los Angeles. He worked for John C. Austin, who de-signed the Griffith Park Observatory among other structures, including the Higgins/Verbeck/Hirsch Mansion soon to be seen. He worked in the office of John Austin from 1917-1919 and opened his own firm in 1922 on Wilshire Boulevard. He was the first African-American to join the American Institute of Architects. Williams was responsible for remodeling the Beverly Hills Hotel in 1947 and 1951, as well as the Ambassador Hotel in 1949. He had an extraordinarily prolific career in Los Angeles and around the world, mostly in Colombia, South America, Mexico, and Canada. The bulk of his work was comprised of residential designs for affluent clients, many in Hancock Park, Beverly Hills, Bel-Air, and Brentwood, although he was commissioned for many commercial projects such as office buildings, hotels, and restaurants. His celebrity clients included Frank Sinatra, Danny Thomas, Lucille Ball and Desi Arnaz, Tyrone Power, and Cary Grant. He died in 1980.

14) Perino's Restaurant, 1963, Paul Williams (remodel), 4118 Wilshire Blvd.

15) Right next to Perino's is the Los Altos Hotel & Apartments, built circa 1926 and designed by Edward B. Rust in the Spanish Colonial Revival style. At one time it was home to William Randolph Hearst, Marion Davies, and Clara Bow. Other celebrities thought to have lived here at one time or another include Judy Garland and Charlie Chaplin. Architect Julia Morgan, designer of Hearst Castle in San Simeon on the central coast of California, designed the apartment for Hearst and Davies. Time and neglect, however, took their toll on this building and in the late 1980s, after the building had been abandoned for ten years, it was condemned and ready for demolition. A group called "Neighborhood Effort" bought the building in 1997. The group was formed after the Northridge earthquake in 1994 with the goal of renovating historically significant buildings and creating affordable housing. It took millions of dollars and one-and-a-half years to complete, but in 1999 the doors opened and there are currently about thirty percent low-income apartments and the rest are market-value apartments. The parking garage was added in the late 1980s. The building has been declared Historic Cultural Monument #311 by the City of Los Angeles and is also listed on the National Register of Historic Places.

15) Los Altos Hotel & Apartments, 1926, Edward B. Rust, 4121 Wilshire Blvd.

Right on Bronson Avenue; Left on 6th Street; Left on Irving Blvd.

16) The house here on the right corner of Irving Boulevard and 6th Street is called the Getty House and was designed in 1920 by the Milwaukee Building Company. It is now the official residence of the mayor of Los Angeles. It is called the Getty House because an employee of the Getty Oil Company, E.D. Buckley, bought the property in 1958. In 1975 the vice president of Getty Oil offered the home to the city if they would use it as the official mayoral residence and call it Getty House in memory of George F. Getty, son of J. Paul Getty. Former mayor Tom Bradley lived in the house for sixteen years. Look ahead a little further to your left and you'll see a better view of the Los Altos Hotel & Apartments.

17) VIEW of Los Altos Hotel & Apartments, 1926, Edward B. Rust, 4121 WILSHIRE BLVD.

 ## Right on Wilshire Blvd.

18) The tall white office building on the right corner is the Harbor Building, built in 1958 by the architectural firm of Brandow & Johnson. It was originally the offices for the Tidewater Oil Company, Getty Oil, and then Harbor Insurance (for which it is named). The building now houses the offices of the L.A. School Board as well as other businesses. This commercial Modern style was popular after World War II. Notice the white marble, metal spandrels, and clean lines of the structure.

16) Getty House (Los Angeles Mayoral Residence), c. 1920, Milwaukee Building Company, 605 SOUTH IRVING BLVD.

18) Harbor Building, 1958, Brandow & Johnson, 4201 WILSHIRE BLVD.

19) On your left is the Dunes Hotel, designed in 1957 by Sam Reisbord. It is a simple, modern design with pure rectilinear and cylindrical geometric forms. The design utilizes brick in an innovative and decorative way, forming a cylinder at the corner with the bricks facing outward to create surface interest.

19) Dunes Hotel, 1957, Sam Reisbord, 4300 WILSHIRE BLVD.

20) On the right, the Washington Mutual Building, originally the Lytton Building, built in 1968 by William Pereira & Associates, is in a style of architecture known to some as Brutalist. There were more buildings in this style created in Europe and this country in the 1950s through the 1970s. The hard block form, undecorated surface, and unfinished-looking concrete quality lend the style this harsh name.

20) Lytton Building (now Washington Mutual Bank), 1968, William Pereira & Associates, 4333 WILSHIRE BLVD.

21) On your left is the Wilshire United Methodist Church, which was designed by Allison & Allison and Austin Whittlesey in 1924 and combines elements of Romanesque and Gothic architecture. The Romanesque characteristics are visible in the entrance's repeated arches, which are also used as decoration at the borders of the structure. On the side of the building are recessed Gothic pointed arches framing rounded arches and columns. The Gothic pointed arch can also be seen in the two flanking front entrances to the church. As is often found in churches, there is also a tall bell tower here. This building is listed as Historic-Cultural Monument #114 by the City of Los Angeles.

21) Wilshire United Methodist Church, 1924, Allison and Allison and Austin Whittlesey, 4350 WILSHIRE BLVD.

22) Scottish Rite Masonic Temple, 1961, Millard Sheets, 4357 WILSHIRE BLVD.

23) Wilshire Ebell Theatre and Club, c. 1924 -7, Hunt & Burns, 4400 WILSHIRE BLVD.

22) On your right, the massive box-like structure is the Scottish Rite Masonic Temple, designed by Millard Sheets, designer of the Home Savings Banks, as well as a fine art painter. Built in 1961, the building is clad in travertine tile and decorated with mosaic tile murals and relief sculpture, to make a strong architectural statement, as the Masonic Temples worldwide are known to do. The relief sculpture on the front of the building depicts builders throughout history. Starting with Imhotep, builder of the ancient pyramids, and ending on the corner with British architect Sir Christopher Wren, designer of St. Paul's Cathedral in London, and George Washington, the country's first president and a member of this organization. It now houses a museum displaying artifacts of the Masons organization which is open to the public.

23) On the left is the Wilshire Ebell Theatre and Club, built circa 1927 by Sumner P. Hunt and Silas R. Burns in the Neo-Classical or European Beaux-Arts style. The Ebell of Los Angeles is a non-profit women's organization founded in 1894, and is one of the nation's oldest and largest women's clubs. Educational and cultural programs are presented here, where luminaries such as Amelia Earhart and Shirley Temple have been received. A large, arched entrance and windows, balustrade railings throughout, a central cartouche above the entrance with the "E" emblem, and a pair of urns above that all contribute to its elegant style. This building is listed as Historic-Cultural Monument #250 by the City of Los Angeles. This location is also listed on the National Register of Historic Places.

Right on Lucerne Blvd.

24) Here on your left is the magnificent Higgins/Verbeck/Hirsch Mansion, completed in 1902 by John C. Austin for Hiram Higgins. It was originally located at 2619 Wilshire Boulevard and moved to this site in the early 1920s. It is in the high style of Victorian architecture. Projecting and curved forms, leaded glass windows of all shapes and sizes, varying roof lines including pyramidal and conical shapes, a barrel-shaped turret on the left side, clapboard siding, and a wrap-around porch are all elements of the Victorian style, still popular here during the turn of the 20th century. Engaged columns, arched windows, and a rusticated stone entrance allude to the European Beaux-Arts style. In the '20s Wilshire Boulevard was being developed as a commercial district and the house was purchased by interior designer Howard Verbeck for use as his show house and personal home. This house is listed as Historic-Cultural Monument #403 by the City of Los Angeles.

24) Higgins/Verbeck/Hirsch Mansion, 1902, John C. Austin, 637 SOUTH LUCERNE BLVD.

25) Interestingly, the green Craftsman style Burgess House on your right was also moved to this site from 608 South St. Andrew's Place, some blocks east of here, by the Kress House Moving Company in 1923 at a cost of $4,000. The receipt for the move was the only paper trail found for this house.

25) Burgess House, c. 1923, (architect unknown), 630 SOUTH LUCERNE BLVD.

Right on 6th Street; Left on Lorraine Blvd.

26) Here on your right, at the corner of Lorraine Boulevard and 6th Street, this brick house designed in a version of English Tudor was designed for Mrs. Frederick Leistikow by the prominent architectural firm of John C. Austin and Frederick M. Ashley at an estimated cost of $81,000. These are the same architects who designed the Griffith Observatory and other structures in the city, including the Higgins/Verbeck/Hirsch Mansion just seen.

26) Leistikow House, 1923, John C. Austin & Frederick M. Ashley, 554 SOUTH LORRAINE BLVD.

27) Coming up on your left, at the northwest corner of 5th Street, is one of the grandest residences in this area. The house is called "Los Tiempos," or "The Times," because it was once owned by the publishers of the *L.A. Times* newspaper, Norman and Dorothy Chandler. Designed by J. Martyn Haenke and W.J. Dodd in 1913 originally for the Janss family, who developed Westwood and Holmby Hills. The Classical Beaux-Arts revival style is characterized by the columns with scrolled capitals, balustrade at the roof, and fanlight windows. Former presidents Kennedy, Nixon, and Johnson all stayed here at one time when the Chandlers lived here. The house was meticulously restored by interior designer Timothy Corrigan in the 1990s.

27) Janss/Chandler House ("Los Tiempos"), 1913, J. Martyn Haenke & W.J. Dodd, 455 SOUTH LORRAINE BLVD.

28) Next, on your left, the impressive white house is the Donovan House, also known as "Sunshine Hall." The home is believed to have been designed circa 1910 by Theodore Eisen of the well-known firm Walker & Eisen, although documents from 1920 list Frank Meline as the architect for alterations and the addition of servants' quarters and a garage. Dr. Harwood Huntington was listed as the owner in 1920. Meline is responsible for numerous residences in Los Angeles and the surrounding areas. This house is a magnificent example of Classical Greek Revival architecture with its front columns, central triangular pediment, and dentil (teeth-like) molding. Resembling a Greek temple, this house is also reminiscent of antebellum houses in the South. Supposedly, the wife of the home's original owner was from the South and it was built this way to remind her of home. This house is listed as Historic-Cultural Monument # 115 by the City of Los Angeles.

28) Donovan House (a.k.a. "Sunshine Hall"), c. 1910, 419 SOUTH LORRAINE BLVD.

29) On your left, at the corner of Lorraine Boulevard and 4th Street, is the Van Nuys House, built in 1898 by architect Frederick Roehrig, who also designed the Hotel Green in Pasadena. This is one of the oldest houses in the area. Isaac Newton Van Nuys was a wheat farmer who had an enormous farm in the San Fernando Valley. The area where the farm once was now bears his name as the City of Van Nuys. His house here was designed in the Shingle Style, which was popular on the East Coast during the late Victorian period, making it somewhat of a rarity here. The style is an offshoot of the Victorian and Colonial styles. The ground level is characteristically constructed of rusticated stone and the upper levels display turrets, eyebrows, many windows, and of course, shingles. This style was the height of fashion in the 1880s. The house was moved to this site in two parts, most likely in the 1920s. It was used in the 2003 movie *Cheaper By the Dozen*.

29) Van Nuys House, 1898, Frederick L. Roehrig, 357 SOUTH LORRAINE BLVD.

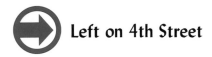 **Left on 4th Street**

You are still in the neighborhood called "Windsor Square." This is the area east of Rossmore Avenue (really Arden Boulevard), north to Beverly Boulevard, south to Wilshire Boulevard, and west of Van Ness Avenue. The area west of Rossmore, which we will soon see is called "Hancock Park."

Windsor Square was developed with the intention of making it the new exclusive area in Los Angeles to succeed the elegant and affluent West Adams district near the University of Southern California (USC), where many affluent Los Angeles people lived at the turn of the 20th century. In the late 1800s the area was originally owned by Canadian Captain John C. Plummer and his wife. In 1911 a group of businessmen called the Windsor Square Investment Company bought 200 acres and this became what is currently known as Windsor Square.

G. Allan Hancock owned most of what was once called Rancho La Brea. La Brea means "tar," and this was the site of numerous oil wells from which Hancock became a wealthy man. After World War I he laid out housing tracts for the subdivision now known as Hancock Park. The actual Hancock County Park is behind the La Brea tar pits and the Los Angeles County Museum of Art, which you will see later. Hancock Park is bounded by Wilshire Boulevard to the south, Melrose Avenue to the north, and from Rossmore Avenue to Highland Avenue to the west.

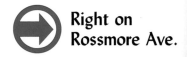 **Right on Rossmore Ave.**

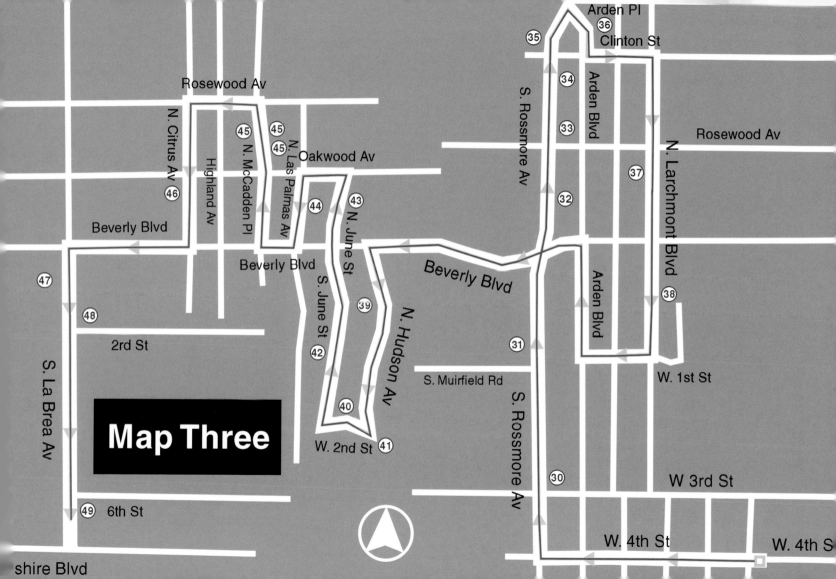

Map Three

Arden Pl
35
36
Clinton St
34
Arden Blvd
33
S. Rossmore Av
Rosewood Av
32
N. Larchmont Blvd
37
Rosewood Av
45
45
45
N. Citrus Av
Highland Av
N. McCadden Pl
N. Las Palmas Av
Oakwood Av
44
43
N. June St
46
Beverly Blvd
Beverly Blvd
Beverly Blvd
38
47
Arden Blvd
48
S. June St
39
31
2rd St
N. Hudson Av
S. Muirfield Rd
42
S. Rossmore Av
40
W. 1st St
W. 2nd St
41
30
W 3rd St
49
6th St
W. 4th St
W. 4th S
shire Blvd

30) The Marlborough School, here on the right corner of Rossmore Avenue and 3rd Street, has been in existence since 1889, but only at this site since 1916. In 1927 John C. Austin and Frederick Ashley designed a structure for the school, but none of it remains. It is a private girls' high school and was recently remodeled in 1997.

31) Here on your left, past Muirfield Street behind the white balustrade railing, is another Greek Revival style house. The fluted columns with scrolled capitals are reminiscent of a Greek temple or Neo-Classical architecture. This house was designed by architect Wallace Neff circa 1960 for a Ralph J. Chandler, perhaps a relative of the *L.A. Times'* Chandlers. Wallace Neff is well known for designing houses in the Spanish Mediterranean style, a far departure from what is seen here.

The Wilshire Country Club, here at the corner of Rossmore Avenue and Beverly Boulevard, opened in 1911. Its golf course jumps across Beverly Boulevard via an underground tunnel and shares its grounds with the backyards of many houses in Hancock Park.

32) Coming up ahead quickly there are a number of notable apartment buildings. The tallest building on your right is the El Royale Apartments, built circa 1920 by William Douglas Lee and home to such stars as George Raft, Loretta Young, and more recently, Uma Thurman and Nicholas Cage. It is an example of a combination of French and Spanish Colonial Revival styles. This building is listed as Historic-Cultural Monument #309 by the City of Los Angeles.

30) Marlborough School, 1927, John C. Austin & Frederick M. Ashley, (since remodeled), 250 SOUTH ROSSMORE AVE.

31) Ralph J. Chandler House, c. 1960, Wallace Neff, 105 NORTH ROSSMORE AVE.

32) El Royale Apartments, c. 1920, William Douglas Lee, 450 NORTH ROSSMORE AVE.

33) Next, coming up quickly on your right just past Rosewood Avenue, is a two-story apartment building in the Art Deco Streamline Moderne style. Called "The Mauretania" after the British ship, the building was designed in 1934 by Milton Black. Resembling a cruise ship with its sweeping, clean lines, it is a shining example of this style. Notice the waterfall-like fins in the front of the building. The spacious apartments have curved walls of glass, casement windows, built-in cabinetry, and period tilework. The building was once owned by the Ahmanson banking family and was where John F. Kennedy stayed when he visited Los Angeles. The typewriter that he used to write a letter to Jackie Robinson is on display in the lobby.

34) Next, on your right, the large white structure is the Ravenswood Apartments. Designed in the Art Deco style in 1930 by Max Maltzman, this was the home of actress Mae West for forty-eight years and was originally owned by Paramount Studios, which is nearby. The stylized floral form decoration on the exterior and ziggurat outline of the windows was typical of the Art Deco style. This building is listed as Historic-Cultural Monument #768 by the City of Los Angeles.

34) Ravenswood Apartments, 1930, Max Maltzman, 570 NORTH ROSSMORE AVE.

33) The Mauretania Apartments, 1934, Milton J. Black, 520-522 NORTH ROSSMORE AVE.

35) Look to your left, at the northwest corner of Rossmore Avenue and Clinton Street, to see the Jester Apartments. The brick building was designed by William Allan & E. Allan Sheet in 1927 in a kind of Neo-Gothic style.

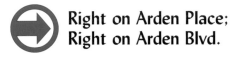

Right on Arden Place;
Right on Arden Blvd.

36) Right here on your left behind the trees is a little box of a house designed by Irving Gill in 1917. The Morgan House is entirely concrete and has a central courtyard. This little house is significant because Irving Gill is credited with simplifying the Spanish Colonial Revival style and creating a truly modern Californian style. Here he took off all ornamentation, leaving the bare concrete structure. Inside, the concrete floors were made with added pigment and then waxed to give a feeling of old leather. Gill worked in Chicago in the office of Sullivan and Adler when Frank Lloyd Wright was also working there. He eventually came west and the bulk of his work is in San Diego, where he died in 1937, but there are other examples in Pasadena, Torrance, and Sierra Madre.

The houses on this street are typical modest California bungalows.

35) Jester Apartments, 1927, William Allan & E. Allan Sheet, 601 North Rossmore Ave.

36) Morgan House, 1917, Irving Gill, 626 North Arden Blvd.

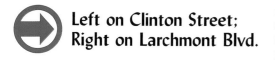

Left on Clinton Street; Right on Larchmont Blvd.

37) Here on your right, past Rosewood Avenue, is the house of the architect Scott Johnson and his family. Johnson's firm, Johnson Fain, has designed a wide range of buildings, from Fox Plaza Tower in Century City to the Opus One Winery in the Napa Valley. The architect's own house was completed in 2001. It was constructed of corrugated steel and channeled glass, is 6,000 square feet in size, and includes a second-floor swim-

ming pool. It is considered by some to be a an abstraction of geometric forms and to be an urban oasis in the middle of the city. One of the best advantages of the house being in a commercial area is the pleasure of walking to the nearby shops and restaurants of Larchmont Village.

38) The Larchmont Boulevard commercial district started to develop in the early 1920s. A streetcar originally ran right down the middle of the street, which was lined with small shops, offices, and restaurants. The small-scale businesses still exist, making this little section of Los Angeles feel like a small town.

38) Larchmont Blvd. Commercial District, c. 1920s, LARCHMONT BLVD.

37) Johnson House, 2001, Scott Johnson, 429 NORTH LARCHMONT BLVD.

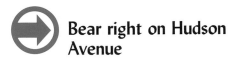

**Right on 1st Street;
Right on Arden Blvd.;
Left on Beverly Blvd.;
Left on Hudson Avenue**

39) Now you are entering Hancock Park proper, west of Rossmore Avenue. Coming up on your right is a wonderful example of English Tudor Revival architecture, based on a 16th century style. The Young House, designed circa 1928 by Roland Coate, is really a magnificent grand home. The proportions suggest a large-scale traditional English manor, and the details have been carried out impeccably. Notice the woodcarving on the trim, leaded glass windows, and chimney pots. (Note: In the 1994 6.8 Northridge Earthquake many chimneys were lost, hence the reinforcements for this one.)

39) Young House, c. 1928, Roland E. Coate, 101 NORTH HUDSON AVE.

Bear right on Hudson Avenue

40) Next, coming up on your right, at the northwest corner of Hudson Avenue and 2nd Street, is a very unique house, especially for this area. The large white structure known as the Smith House was designed in 1930 by Clarence J. Smale. It is truly a breath of fresh air in this neighborhood full of Revival styles. This house in the Art Deco style is true to the time it was built. The Art Deco style flourished in Los Angeles in the 1920s and '30s, but mostly in commercial and multi-unit dwellings, so to find this single family home here is truly rare. Some of it is hidden by foliage, but look at the leaded stained glass windows and the roofline for some exquisite details.

40) Smith House, 1929-30, Clarence J. Smale, 191 NORTH HUDSON AVE.

41) Diagonally across from the Smith House is a much newer house, notable for its architect. The two-story house with second story balcony is the Berman/Bloch House, a modestly designed residence in contrast to so many of the others in this area. It was designed in 1957 by important architect Wallace Neff. Neff created much of his work in Pasadena and Beverly Hills in the Spanish Mediterranean style. This mid-20th century home is very different, and thought of as Panamanian in style with open spaces in back facing the golf course and a second story recessed balcony to catch breezes.

41) Berman/Bloch House, 1957, Wallace Neff, 200 SOUTH HUDSON AVE.

➡ Right on 2nd Street;
Right on June Street

42) Coming up on your left are two houses owned by the Turkish Consulate General. The first house is called the Baydar-Demir House and the next is called the Arikan House. Hancock Park and its surrounding areas are home to a number of foreign consulates including the Korean, German, Belgian, Mexican, Canadian, and British consulates. Look for the flags of those countries in front of the houses to find them.

42) Turkish Consulate Houses, (Arikan House & Baydar-Demir House), 153 South June Street

43) La Casa de las Campanas, 1928, Lester Scherer (Lucile Mead), 350 North June Street

➡ Cross Beverly Blvd.

43) Next, coming up on your right behind the lushly and densely landscaped front yard, is La Casa de Las Campanas, or The House of the Bells. Built in 1928 by the Mead family, architect Lester Scherer based the home's design on sketches by daughter Lucile Mead, who at 23 years old was an aspiring artist and designer. Designed in the Spanish Colonial Revival style, it has a three-story tower housing four enormous bells. One of the oldest bells in California, dating from 1790, is here on a candelabra in the center of the home, which is now owned by movie producers. This house is listed as Historic-Cultural Monument #239 by the City of Los Angeles.

**Left on Oakwood Avenue;
Left on Las Palmas Avenue**

44) Coming up here on your left is another house designed by Paul Williams. The Gabriel Duque House was built in 1932 and has elements of the French Regency style, which was the architect's signature style. Graceful and delicate lines, a steep roof line, and large arched windows are characteristic of this style.

44) Gabriel Duque House, 1932, Paul Williams, 340 North Las Palmas Ave.

**Right on Beverly Blvd.;
Right on McCadden Place**

45) Past Oakwood Avenue on the right and left are three more houses designed by Paul Williams. The Banning Houses were built in 1929 (one here at 425 and two others on the right at 426 and 432) and were at one time all part of the same house. The original Banning house was located in the Adams area of Los Angeles, near the University of Southern California. Some recycled materials from the original house were used to build these three smaller houses. The Banning family was in the business of shipping, ports, and stagecoaches. When it became fashionable to move to this part of Los Angeles they had the three houses built. The one on your left was for William Phineas Banning and his wife, and the houses across the street were for brother Joseph B. Banning, Jr. and his widowed mother (432), and uncle Captain William Banning (426).

45) Banning Houses, 1929, Paul Williams, 425 North McCadden, 426 & 432 NORTH McCADDEN

 Left on Rosewood Avenue; Cross Highland Avenue; Left on Citrus Avenue; Pass Oakwood Avenue

46) Next, coming up on your right is another rarity in this area. The Beckman House was built in 1938 by modernist architect Gregory Ain and is quite different from most of the other houses in the neighborhood with its flat roof, large clerestory windows, rectilinear form, and geometric patterned wrought iron gate. Ain was known as a California Modernist architect although he was born in Pennsylvania. He designed single-family homes, like this one, and multi-unit dwellings in various areas in Los Angeles. The Mar Vista Housing on the west side of town, near Venice, was designed by Ain after World War II and was recently designated a Historic Preservation Overlay Zone (HPOZ). It comprises fifty-two homes designed in Ain's distinctive Modern or International style.

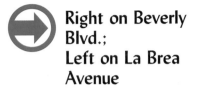

Right on Beverly Blvd.; Left on La Brea Avenue

47) La Brea Avenue was created as a commercial district that was first developed in the 1920s and '30s. A notable building in the Italian/Spanish Revival style is coming up on your right. The two-story Tipton Building (now Amalfi Restaurant) was built in 1928 and designed by E.B. Watson as shops. Notice the arches and twisted mini columns.

48) An Art Deco building is coming up on your left. The Art: 170 Building was designed by Herbert Nelson circa 1930. It has simple streamline Art Deco details.

Once known for its large selection of car dealerships, La Brea Avenue has many Art Deco and Spanish Colonial Revival style buildings, popular styles of the 1920s.

46) Beckman House, 1938, Gregory Ain, 357 NORTH CITRUS AVE.

47) Tipton Building (now Amalfi Restaurant), c. 1928, E.B. Watson, 143 NORTH LA BREA AVE.

48) Art: 170 Building, c. 1930, Herbert E. Nelson, 170 SOUTH LA BREA AVE.

49) Another building of note is on your left behind the trees. Past 6th Street, look for the gray brick building with the tall box-shaped tower (or campanile) in back decorated with applied stars. LaBrea Bakery and Campanile Restaurant have been here since 1989, but the building was originally owned by the second wife of Charlie Chaplin, Lita Grey Chaplin, and was designed by architect Roy Seldon Price in 1928 as a collection of shops. It was a mini-mall of sorts, featuring a cigar shop, a beauty shop, and others. The mini-mall was transformed into a restaurant by architect Josh Schweitzer, husband of restaurateur Mary Sue Milliken, in 1989.

49) Lita Grey Chaplin Building, (now Campanile Restaurant), 1928, Roy Seldon Price, Remodel 1989, Schweitzer BIM, 624 SOUTH LA BREA AVE.

 **Right on Wilshire Blvd.**

The Miracle Mile was developed by A.W. Ross in the early 1920s. Originally part of a bean field, it extends along Wilshire Boulevard from LaBrea Avenue to Fairfax Avenue. It was one of the first commercial areas to provide parking in the back of stores. It is now part of the Miracle Mile Historic District, declared as such by the City of Los Angeles. There are excellent examples of Art Deco architecture lining the street.

Some say it was called the "Miracle Mile" because of the speed with which it was built. Others say it was because it was "a miracle" to get people all the way up here to shop from Downtown, which at the time was the only place to shop in Los Angeles. Still others claim that Ross's exaggerated talk and enthusiasm for the development made it sound as if it were a miracle. The Art Deco style was dominant here, inspired by "The Exposition of Industrial and Decorative Arts" that took place in Paris in the early 1920s and heavily influenced designers, architects, and builders. It was an international art movement and everything from jewelry and fashion to architecture reflected this style.

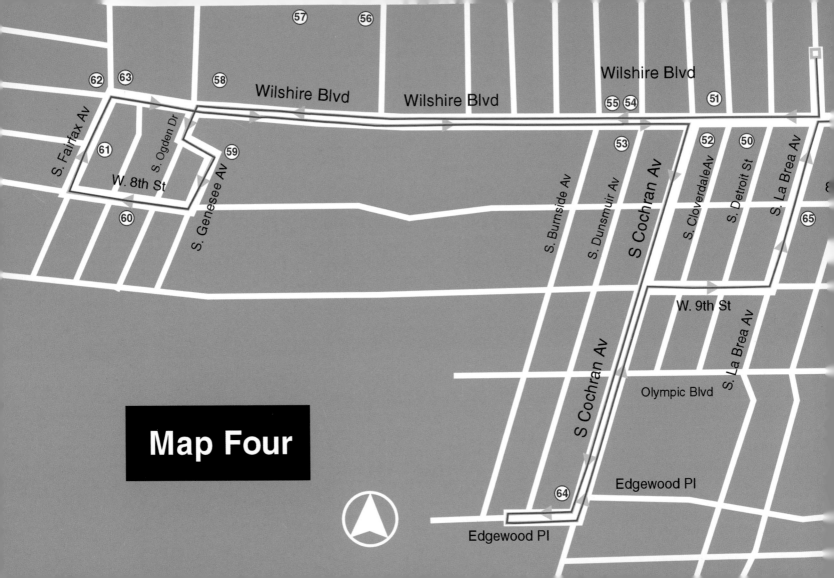

Map Four

57 56

62 63 58

Wilshire Blvd

Wilshire Blvd

Wilshire Blvd

55 54

51

S. Farfax Av

61

S. Ogden Dr

59

53

52

50

S. Burnside Av

S. Dunsmuir Av

S Cochran Av

S. Cloverdale Av

S. Detroit St

S. La Brea Av

65

60

W. 8th St

S. Genesee Av

W. 9th St

S Cochran Av

S. La Brea Av

Olympic Blvd

64

Edgewood Pl

Edgewood Pl

50) On your left, between Detroit Street and Cloverdale Avenue, look for the giant-sized black glass camera. The Darkroom (now the Conga room) was designed in 1938 by Marcus Miller and is an early example of Programmatic architecture. Structures designed in this type of architectural style were meant to catch your eye as you drive by. Here, the building in the shape of a 35 mm camera was, fittingly, originally a camera and film-processing store. Programmatic style buildings take on the shape of the object they are trying to promote and become a street advertisement. The style is perfect for the car culture. This facade is listed as Historic-Cultural Monument #451 by the City of Los Angeles.

51) The Wilshire Beauty Supply store, on the right corner of Cloverdale Avenue, was built circa 1930-35 and designed as stores by Norstrom & Anderson.

51) Stores (now Wilshire Beauty Supply), c. 1930-35, Norstrom & Anderson, 5401 WILSHIRE BLVD.

52) Across the street on your left, between Cloverdale Avenue and Cochran Avenue, is the recently-restored Dominguez-Wilshire Building. It was originally designed as a department store in 1930 by Morgan, Walls and Clements. The very elegant and upscale Art Deco style lobby is still intact. The restoration of this building was recognized with an award from the Los Angeles Conservancy. This building is listed as Historic-Cultural Monument #2170 by the City of Los Angeles.

50) The Darkroom (now Conga Room), 1938, Marcus P. Miller, 5370 WILSHIRE BLVD.

52) Dominguez-Wilshire Building, 1930, Morgan, Walls & Clements, 5410 Wilshire Blvd.

53) Next, on your left between Burnside and Dunsmuir Avenues, Desmonds Department Store/Silverwoods once occupied the Wilshire Tower, which was designed by architect Gilbert Stanley Underwood in 1928-29. He also designed the Federal Courthouse in Downtown L.A., which can be seen on the DOWNTOWN tour. Designed in the Art Deco style, the tall shaft of the tower is an early version of a skyscraper as it rests on the block-long base. The second floor now houses Ace Gallery, the largest contemporary art gallery in Los Angeles. Desmonds was originally located Downtown and was one of the first stores to move to the Miracle Mile. It was also one of the first to have the parking lot in the rear of the building, which at the time was an innovation. This building is listed as Historic-Cultural Monument #332 by the City of Los Angeles.

53) Desmonds Department Store/ Silverwoods (a.k.a. Wilshire Tower), 1928-29, Gilbert Stanley Underwood, 5514 WILSHIRE BLVD.

54) Across the street on your right, at the corner of Dunsmuir Avenue, notice the building with the Neo-Classical fluted columns in front. Originally built as a store, then a bank, the Korean Cultural Center was designed circa 1929 in a mixture of Art Deco and Neo-Classical styles. The relief sculpture frieze at the top is decorated with abstracted and geometrized foliage and resembles a quasi Pre-Columbian style of decoration, but is actually more in the Art Deco style. This building is listed as Historic-Cultural Monument #2164 by the City of Los Angeles.

54) Store/Bank (now Korean Cultural Center), c. 1929, (architect unknown), 5505 WILSHIRE BLVD.

55) The El Rey Theatre, two doors down on your right, is a flamboyant example of the Art Deco style. Designed circa 1936 by Clifford Balch, it displays the exuberance of Art Deco with stylized floral forms and curvilinear shapes. The terrazzo floor in front is an excellent example of the use of this material in Art Deco buildings. This building is listed as Historic-Cultural Monument #520 by the City of Los Angeles.

55) El Rey Theatre, c. 1936, Clifford Balch, 5517 WILSHIRE BLVD.

56) Coming up next on Wilshire Boulevard is "Museum Row," starting with the George C. Page Museum of La Brea Discoveries on your right just past Curson Avenue, behind the La Brea Tar Pits. La Brea is the Spanish word for tar and the tar pits are the location of 40,000-year-old prehistoric fossilized bones. Hancock County Park is also here, on land that once belonged to the Hancock Family.

57) Next is the Japanese Pavilion, part of the Los Angeles County Museum of Art (LACMA), which was designed by Bart Prince and the late Bruce Goff in 1988.

58) Next is the Los Angeles County Museum of Art, originally built in 1964 by William Pereira & Associates, with a later expansion in 1986 by Hardy, Holzman & Pfeiffer. The Los Angeles County Museum Sculpture Garden and the Southwest Museum at LACMA in the former May Company Building add to the composition of the museum campus. On the left across the street is the Craft and Folk Art Museum.

56) George C. Page Museum (La Brea Tar Pits), 1976, Thornton & Fagan Associates, 5801 Wilshire Blvd.

57) Japanese Pavilion, 1988, Bart Prince & Bruce Goff, 5905 Wilshire Blvd.

58) Los Angeles County Museum of Art, 1964, William Pereira & Associates, Expansion, 1986, Hardy, Holzman, Pfeiffer, 5801 Wilshire Blvd.

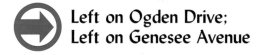

Left on Ogden Drive; Left on Genesee Avenue

59) You will take a little turn here to see this gem of an Art Deco apartment building. No original building permit was found for this building, but it was probably built circa 1925-30. The pastel paint colors serve to enhance the architectural detailing.

59) Art Deco Apartments, c. 1925-1930, (architect unknown), 724 SOUTH GENESEE AVE.

 Right on 8th Street

60) Next, all in white is one of Austrian-born architect Rudolf M. Schindler's masterpieces, the Buck House, built in 1934. The flat roof, bands of windows, and lack of surface ornamentation are the signature visual characteristics of Schindler's work. Displaying rectilinear forms and sculptural abstraction, Schindler was concerned with spatial relationships, as we can see in this structure, with drama occurring where volumes intersect and the

play of light upon these shapes creates a changing interior dynamic. The clerestory windows provide a way for light to enter, yet are high enough to allow for privacy. A three-bedroom house with garage is on the ground level and a smaller one-bedroom apartment is on the upper level. The back of the house opens onto a very private grassy courtyard. This house is listed as Historic-Cultural Monument #122 by the City of Los Angeles.

60) Buck House, 1934, Rudolf M. Schindler, 805 SOUTH GENESEE

 **Continue on 8th Street**

On your right are the white spiral parking garage ramps at the back of the Peterson Automotive Museum, which opened in 1994.

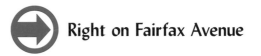 **Right on Fairfax Avenue**

61) Originally built as a Japanese department store in 1961, the Seibu department store was designed by Welton Becket & Associates, the same architects of the Capitol Records Tower in Hollywood and seen on the HOLLYWOOD tour. From the 1970s to the '80s Orbach's department store occupied this building and in 1994 architect Mark Whipple of The Russell Group reconfigured the structure into the current museum. An expansion was planned to add more space for the display of automobiles and gathering spaces, but has not yet begun as of 2004.

61) Seibu Department Store(now Peterson Automotive Museum), 1961, Welton Becket & Associates, 6060 WILSHIRE BLVD.

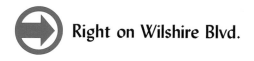

Right on Wilshire Blvd.

62) On the northwest corner of Wilshire Boulevard and Fairfax Avenue where Johnie's restaurant now stands, was originally a diner called Romeo's Times Square, designed by Louis Armet & Eldon Davis in 1956. Typical of the 1950s diner-style design, these architects also designed Pann's restaurant at LaCienega and LaTijera Boulevards, Conrad's Drive-In (now Astro Family Restaurant) in Silver Lake, and the Norm's restaurants around Los Angeles.

62) Romeo's Times Square (now Johnie's), 1956, Louis Armet & Eldon Davis, 6101 WILSHIRE BLVD.

63) At the northeast corner of Wilshire Boulevard and Fairfax Avenue, the building with the gold tiled cylindrical column was intended to resemble a perfume bottle, and now houses the Southwest Museum at LACMA and LACMA West. It was originally the May Company Department Store, built circa 1940 by Albert C. Martin and Samuel A. Marx in the Late Art Deco Streamline Moderne style. It was purchased by LACMA in 1994 and absorbed into their campus. This building is listed as Historic-Cultural Monument #566 by the City of Los Angeles.

63) May Company Department Store (now LACMA West-Southwest Museum), c. 1940, Albert C. Martin, Sr. & Samuel A. Marx, 6067 WILSHIRE BLVD.

You will again be on the Miracle Mile and have another chance to see the buildings from the other side of the street.

 Right on Cochran Avenue; Cross Olympic Blvd.

64) Coming up on your right, just past and across from Edgewood Place, is another building designed by Rudolf M. Schindler. The Mackey Apartments, built in 1939 and restored in 1994, are now owned by the MAK Center, an Austrian cultural organization. Visiting artists and architects live here on a temporary basis. The front facade is a flat plane with various-sized windows and walls (voids and solids) creating an abstract composition similar to that of a Piet Mondrian painting. There are clerestory windows, built-in furniture, outdoor terraces, and multi levels within the apartments of the original four units. Part of Schindler's plan was this enclosure of hedges in front, which provides a front yard for the building.

64) Mackey Apartments, 1939, Rudolf M. Schindler, Restored 1994, 1137 SOUTH COCHRAN AVE.

 Right on Edgewood Place; Make a U-turn; Left on Cochran Avenue; Cross Olympic Blvd.

There are a variety of architectural styles on this street, with apartment buildings mixed in with single-family residences. Look directly in front of you in the distance and you should be able to see the Hollywood sign perched on Mount Lee.

 Right on 9th Street; Left on La Brea Avenue

65) Coming up on your right, at the corner of 8th Street, is the Firestone Building. Built in 1937 by R.E. Ward, the exterior surface has a quilted pattern appearance. It is made of panels of sheet metal for a look that conveys strength and endurance. A wide, overhanging roof provides lighting and shelter from the elements. This garage has been operational since 1937.

65) Firestone Building, 1937, R.E. Ward, 800 SOUTH LA BREA AVE.

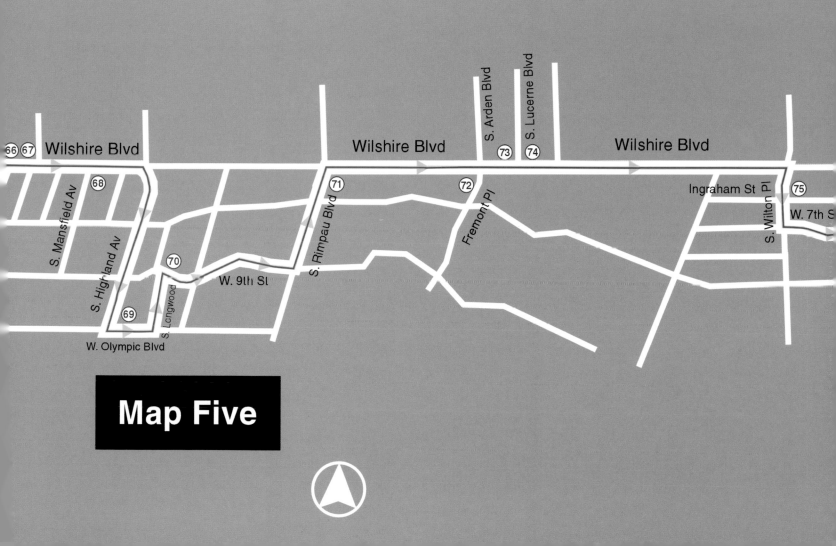

Map Five

66) On the northeast corner of Wilshire Boulevard and La Brea Avenue is the Wilson Building, long-known as the Mutual of Omaha Building because they were once tenants and had a big sign at the top, where the Samsung sign now is. Built in 1930 by Meyer & Holler, who also designed the Chinese and Egyptian Theaters in Hollywood, this building is a departure from their theater designs, as would be fitting of a serious office building built at the time when the Art Deco style was *en vogue*.

67) Directly next to the Wilson Building, the black and gold building is the Kohram Building, built in 1929 by Morgan, Walls & Clements (whose work you have seen earlier and will see again on this tour). Beautiful black terra cotta tiles and gold trim accentuate the sleekness of the Art Deco style here. Once housing a bank, a 2004 renovation has transformed the building into office space. The interior has been lovingly restored, maintaining the original Art Deco decorative metal work and light fixtures. The original vault now serves as a conference room.

68) On your right, at the southeast corner of Mansfield Avenue and Wilshire Boulevard, is another Art Deco building. Originally built as a movie theater in 1929, it is now home to the Christian Oasis Center. The facade has been altered with the addition of large glass block walls, but the Art Deco styling remains.

68) Movie Theatre (now Oasis Christian Church Center), 1929, (architect unknown), 5110 WILSHIRE BLVD.

66) Wilson Building, Mutual of Omaha (now Samsung Building), 1930, Meyer & Holler, 5225 WILSHIRE BLVD.

67) Kohram Building, Security First National Bank of Los Angeles, 1929, Morgan, Walls & Clements, 5209 WILSHIRE BLVD.

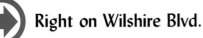

Right on Wilshire Blvd.

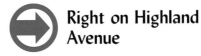

Right on Highland Avenue

69) Look to your left, at the northeast corner of Highland Avenue and Olympic Boulevard, and you will see a very unique-looking residence, quite different from the other houses on the street. Called the "off-use" House, it was built in 2002 by the architects/owners PXS, Linda Pollari and Robert Somol. Created using galvanized sheet metal and structural steel, stucco, wood, and glass, it has a strong street presence. Inside it is 1,826 square feet with large open spaces that combine a kitchen, lounge, and gallery with no interior doors. Bedrooms and bathrooms are enclosed for privacy. The location on a very busy traffic intersection presented challenges. The design is meant to embrace its relationship with the busy street. The low horizontal slit windows let in light as well as produce a changing view throughout the day, mimicking the feeling of the cars whizzing by. The house has a linear, graphic quality amidst wild looking landscaping, creating a dynamic contrast.

69) "off-use" House, 2002, PXS, 950 SOUTH HIGHLAND AVE.

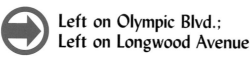

**Left on Olympic Blvd.;
Left on Longwood Avenue**

This area is known as Brookside. Originally called Windsor Crest, it was first part of the Rancho Las Cienegas (Ranch of the Marshland), one of the many Mexican ranchos in southern California. It was named for a natural underground stream that the developers planned around. They wanted to preserve some of the natural features of the land, so the roads are curved and meandering and the stream is on both sides of Longwood Avenue. The stream is impossible to see from the street, but sometimes you can hear it.

Straight ahead of you...

70) The next house you will see is quite imaginative and fantastic. The Chateau LeMoine was built in 1925 by architect Earl LeMoine, who lived here until 1954. It is a fantasy structure designed in the French Normandy style and believed to be a replica of a chateau in Quebec, Canada. Notice the checkerboard decoration, irregularly shaped windows, and conical turrets. Gothic pointed arches are also used here, and a quasi half-timber facade alludes to the French Normandy style. This style was very popular during the 1920s and 1930s all over Los Angeles.

This area has an abundance of houses deigned in various Revival styles.

70) Chateau LeMoine, 1925, Earl LeMoine, 846 SOUTH LONGWOOD AVE.

**Right on 9th Street,
Left on Rimpau Blvd.**

48

71) Right here, on the right corner of Rimpau and Wilshire Boulevards, is the Farmer's Insurance Group Building, originally built in 1937 by Walker & Eisen, with architect Claud Beelman consulting. Albert R. Walker & Percy Eisen designed many buildings in the Los Angeles area, including the Regent Beverly Wilshire Hotel in Beverly Hills, the Fine Arts Building in Downtown L.A., and the Taft Building in Hollywood. This building was originally just three stories high and, as a result, the executive offices are on the third floor. The expansion, which occurred years later, is seamless. The elegant Late Art Deco style is pared down here and given an understated insurance-company look. Some of the most striking elements are the black glass casement windows which are angled outward – a seemingly small detail, but one that has great effect. At the very top, above the main entrance, is a single scrolled palm leaf punctuating the top of the building.

Above and left:
71) Farmer's Insurance Group Building, 1937, Walker & Eisen with Claud Beelman (consulting architect), John Fortune & Associates (expansion), 4680 Wilshire Blvd.

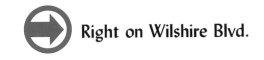

Right on Wilshire Blvd.

72) On your right, notice the gates to Fremont Place. They were designed in 1911 by Martyn Haenke, the same architect who designed the house called "Los Tiempos," seen earlier, as the entrance to a private community. Muhammad Ali once lived here, as did Mary Pickford in the early days of Fremont Place.

72) Fremont Place Entrance Gates, 1911, Martyn Haenke, Corner Wilshire Blvd. & Fremont Place

73) On your left is the Japanese style Hon Michi Los Angeles Shutchosho Temple, built in 1984 by architect Obayashi. It is a church for a religion headquartered in Osaka, Japan, called Ten Rikyo. The structure is of typical Japanese form and sits atop a small rise with landscaped gardens. It is open to the public from 8am-5pm.

73) Hon-Michi Los Angeles Shutchosho, 1984, Obayashi, 4431 WILSHIRE BLVD.

74) The Scottish Rite Masonic Temple on your left, 1961, with relief sculpture depicting historic builders and architects.

74) Scottish Rite Masonic Temple, 1961, Millard Sheets, 4357 WILSHIRE BLVD.

 Right on Wilton Place

75) On your left, at the corner of Ingraham Street and Wilton Place, is the Korean Youth Community Center designed in the Deconstructivist Post-Modern style. It was built in 1992 by Hak Sik Son and is an example of how this style incorporates industrial materials into the design.

75) Korean Youth Community Center, 1992, Hak Sik Son, (Ko-Am Construction), 680 SOUTH WILTON PLACE (3987 INGRAHAM STREET)

Now you'll have another chance to see what you saw before on this stretch of Wilshire Boulevard.

Again on your right, the Wilshire Ebell Theatre, 1924, by Hunt and Burns in the Beaux-Arts style.

Also on your right, the Wilshire United Methodist Church, 1924, by Allison & Allison, combing Romanesque and Gothic architecture.

Again on your left, you'll see the Washington Mutual Building, originally the Lytton Building, designed by William Pereira in 1968.

Also look for the Los Altos Hotel & Apartments, 1926, in the Spanish Colonial Revival style.

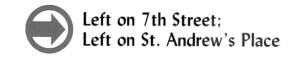 **Left on 7th Street;
Left on St. Andrew's Place**

Wilshire Blvd

S. Oxford Av

S. Serrano Av

S. Hobart Blvd

S. Harvard Blvd

S. Kingsley Dr

S. Normandie Av

S. Mariposa Av

S. Alexandria Av

S. Kenmore Av

S. Berendo St

S. New Hampshire Av

(77)

(79)

(81)

(82)

(83)

(84)

(85)

(88)

(87)

(76)

(78)

(80)

Wilshire Blvd

(86)

(89)

(90)

Wilshire Blvd

(91)

W. 7th St

S. Saint Andrews Pl

Western Av

S. Westmoreland Av

Wilshire Pl

Map Six

76) Here on your right, at the southeast corner of Ingraham Street and St. Andrew's Place, are the St. Andrew's Apartments, remodeled from an older building in 1992 by Kanner Architects. Called the "Swiss cheese" building, bright colors and circular cutouts and windows make it whimsical and fun.

77) Directly in front of you is a jewel to behold — The Wilshire Professional Building, designed in 1929 by Arthur E. Harvey, whose work was seen at the beginning of this tour. Striking in scale, it is a marvelous example of the elaborate Art Deco style, here without exterior color. It is full of geometrized foliage and scrolling decoration, with a cap at the top. Unfortunately, the decoration of the first floor has been obscured with signage.

76) St. Andrew's Apartments, 1992, Kanner Architects, 686 SOUTH ST. ANDREWS PLACE

77) Wilshire Professional Building, 1929, Arthur E. Harvey, 3875 WILSHIRE BLVD.

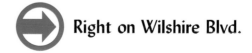 **Right on Wilshire Blvd.**

78) On the right corner, here at Western Avenue, the tall tower covered in green glazed terra cotta tiles is the Pellisier Building, home of the Wiltern Theatre. The building was designed by Morgan, Walls & Clements in 1930-31 in the elaborate Art Deco Zig-Zag Moderne style. The glazed terra cotta tiles were manufactured by Gladding-McBean, and Anthony B. Heinsbergen created the beautiful interiors. This building was in terrible disrepair until Brenda Levin & Associates restored it in 1985. The offices of the L.A. Chapter of the American Institute of Architects are in this building and wonderful concerts are held here in the theater in an intimate setting. This building is listed as Historic-Cultural Monument #118 by the City of Los Angeles. This location is also listed on the National Register of Historic Places.

79) On your left, at the northeast corner of Oxford Street and Wilshire Boulevard, is the Ahmanson Center Building (now Wilshire Colonnade), designed in 1971 by Edward Durrell Stone Associates. The tall whitish structure is comprised of two carbon copy buildings, each with concave walls, which form a central plaza and fountain. The vertical glass bands of windows are capped by a flat roof with rectangular-shaped perforations that draw the eye upwards. On the ground floor is an arched colonnade encircling the plaza. It is a very elegant office building, once owned by the Ahmanson Family, who owned Home Savings banks.

79) Ahmanson Center Building (now Wilshire Colonnade), 1971, Edward Durrell Stone Associates, 3701 WILSHIRE BLVD.

78) Pellisier Building (Wiltern Theatre), 1930-31, Morgan, Walls & Clements, Restored 1985, Levin & Associates, 3790 WILSHIRE BLVD.

80) On the right, directly opposite from the Ahmanson Center Building, is the Beneficial Plaza (now Wilshire Park Place) designed by Skidmore, Owings & Merrill in 1967. With its square sectioned windows the structure resembles a honeycomb. (No doubt, with busy office workers inside.) The same architectural firm that designed this building also designed Chicago's Sears Tower and John Hancock Center, and the Lever House in New York.

81) Next, to your left, on the northeast corner of Hobart Boulevard, is the massive Wilshire Boulevard Temple, designed by Abraham Adelman & others circa 1928. Its design shows the influences of Byzantine architecture complete with dome and striped masonry pattern. Inside there are multi-colored mosaics, inlaid gold, and black marble. This building is listed as Historic-Cultural Monument #116 by the City of Los Angeles.

82) Continuing on your left, at the corner between Harvard Street and Kingsley Drive, is St. Basil's Roman Catholic Church, designed in 1974 by Albert C. Martin & Associates. It is a mass of vertical sculptural forms interspersed with vertical sections of stained glass. The church is very sparse and modern inside, with sculptures by Herb Goldman. This relatively young structure replaced an older one.

80) Beneficial Plaza (now Wilshire Park Place), 1967, Skidmore, Owings & Merrill, 3700 WILSHIRE BLVD.

81) Wilshire Blvd. Temple, c. 1928, Abraham A. Adelman, S. Tilden Norton, and David C. Allison, 3663 WILSHIRE BLVD.

82) St. Basil's Roman Catholic Church, 1974, Albert C. Martin & Associates, 3611 WILSHIRE BLVD.

Along this strip of Wilshire Boulevard and even further west there are quite a few churches and temples. When the city began to expand westward from Downtown in the 1920s many of the religious organizations also decided to move to where land was cheaper and bigger structures could be built.

83) Again on your left, at the corner of Normandie Avenue is the Wilshire Christian Church, designed by Robert Orr in 1927. It was designed in the Neo-Romanesque or Romanesque Revival style and constructed of poured-in-place concrete. The central stained glass rose window is a copy of the one in Rheims Cathedral in France and was produced here by the Judson Studios. This building is listed as Historic-Cultural Monument #209 by the City of Los Angeles.

84) The massive office building on your left, set back from the street at the corner of Mariposa Avenue, is the Equitable Life Building, designed in 1969 by Welton Becket & Associates, whose work you have seen before in the Seibu Department Store (now Peterson Automotive Museum). The visual emphasis is on the verticality of the structure, giving it a sense of enormity and strength. The monolithic structure is one of the tallest buildings here.

83) Wilshire Christian Church, 1927, Robert H. Orr, 634 South Normandie Ave.

84) Equitable Life Building, 1969, Welton Becket & Associates, 3435 WILSHIRE BLVD.

85) One of the original Brown Derby restaurants was located here, on the left corner at Alexandria Avenue, but has not survived intact. A minimall has replaced it, however, there is a "derby hat" shaped restaurant in the corner on the second floor. There were originally four Brown Derby restaurants that were owned by actress Gloria Swanson's second husband. The restaurant served as a Hollywood hangout, attracting friends of Gloria Swanson and other celebrities, as well as tourists hoping to see celebrities. The Cobb Salad originated at this restaurant. It was created by manager, Robert Cobb, for his wife.

85) Location of original Brown Derby Restaurant, CORNER OF ALEXANDRIA AVE. & WILSHIRE BLVD.

86) On your right, at the corner of Alexandria Avenue, is the Ambassador Hotel & Coconut Grove Club, designed in 1921 by Myron Hunt, who also designed the Huntington Estate in San Marino, near Pasadena. The Ambassador Hotel was frequently the winter home for families like the Duponts and the Vanderbilts. The hotel hosted many presidents including Hoover and Nixon, but was also the scene of the infamous assassination of Robert F. Kennedy by Sirhan Sirhan in 1968. This section of Wilshire Boulevard has been named the Robert F. Kennedy Memorial Parkway. The Coconut Grove nightclub saw many movie stars in its heyday, including Charlie Chaplin, Barbara Stanwyck, and Jean Harlow to name a few. It was also the location for many of the Academy Awards presentations. At one time real estate developer Donald Trump purchased it and planned to build the world's tallest skyscraper, but that plan never materialized. The Los Angeles Unified School District acquired it and will be building a school here as of 2005.

86) Ambassador Hotel & Cocoanut Grove Club, 1921, Myron Hunt, 3400 WILSHIRE BLVD.

87) Robert F. Kennedy Memorial Parkway

88) Across the street, at the northwest corner of Kenmore Avenue, the Gaylord Apartments were designed in 1922 by Walker & Eisen as a hotel residence and named after Henry Gaylord Wilshire, who developed this area. The large brick building was one of the tallest in the area when it was first built. The lobby has coffered ceilings and terrazzo floors. Notice the Neo-Classical details gracing the surface of the building around the main entrance. Squared off columns in relief, or pilasters, are crowned with Corinthian columns topped by a border of dentil molding, all adding a bit of grandeur to the apartment building. Next-door, The Bounty restaurant/bar has a door that opens directly into the lobby.

89) On your right, at the southeast corner of Berendo Street, is a brick building with white Neo-Classical decoration. The Talmadge apartment building was financed by silent screen star Norma Talmadge in 1923 and designed by Aleck Curlett & Claud Beelman, like a New York apartment building. The interior lobby has a Wedgwood like frieze crowning the ceiling. Norma Talmadge did live here for a time, but she also had other homes in Los Angeles, one of which can be seen on the SILVER LAKE tour. Some of the apartments are 3,000 squre feet with eight bedrooms and maid's quarters. This was, and still is, considered to be grand apartment living. One of the special features is a doorman and valet parking.

90) Next, on your right, at the southeast corner of New Hampshire Avenue, is the I. Magnin Building (now Wilshire Galleria), designed in 1938 by Myron Hunt & H.C. Chambers. Once a very elegant Late Art Deco style department store sheathed in black granite and white marble, it remains a retail store. Myron Hunt also designed the Ambassador Hotel further back on Wilshire Boulevard. This location is listed as Historic-Cultural Monument #534 by the City of Los Angeles.

90) I. Magnin Building (now Wilshire Galleria), 1938, Myron Hunt & H.C. Chambers, 3240 WILSHIRE BLVD.

88) Gaylord Apartments, 1922, Walker & Eisen, 3355 WILSHIRE BLVD.

89) The Talmadge Apartments, 1923, Aleck Curlett & Claud Beelman, 3278 WILSHIRE BLVD.

 Just past Westmoreland Avenue, turn right on Wilshire Place

91) Towering on your right, on the south side of the street between Westmoreland Avenue and Wilshire Place, is the famed Bullock's Wilshire Department Store (now Southwestern Law Library). Designed in 1929 by John and Donald Parkinson in the Art Deco Moderne style, it is a monumental building with its tall tower. These architects also designed Union Station in Downtown and many other buildings in L.A. Bullock's Wilshire was *the* elegant place to shop in the area and was built to accommodate the shoppers from Hancock Park and Windsor Square. The exteriors are clad in copper and glazed terra cotta decoration and the interiors were considered to be the height of elegance, with streamline stainless steel and marble. Many movie stars shopped here, including Marlene Dietrich. Attached to the back of the building is a porte cochere, which is significant because this store was designed for people to arrive by their own car and not necessarily by streetcar. One could drive up and enter the store, protected from the elements by the porte cochere. A fresco mural painted by Herman Sachs titled "The Spirit of Transportation" depicts transportation of the 1920s and is on the underside of the structure. The mural was restored in 1973 by Anthony Heinsbergen. Southwestern Law School purchased the building in 1994. The architectural firm of Altoon & Porter restored it to house the school's library, which moved into the building in 1997. We are lucky that this building has been respectfully restored to the architect's original vision. It is a remarkable vestige to the elegant stores of the Art Deco age, and is an excellent example of adaptive reuse. This building is listed as Historic-Cultural Monument #56 by the City of Los Angeles. It is also listed on the National Register of Historic Places.

91) Bullock's Wilshire Department Store (now Southwestern Law Library), 1929, John & Donald Parkinson, Restored 1997, Altoon & Porter, 3050 WILSHIRE BLVD.

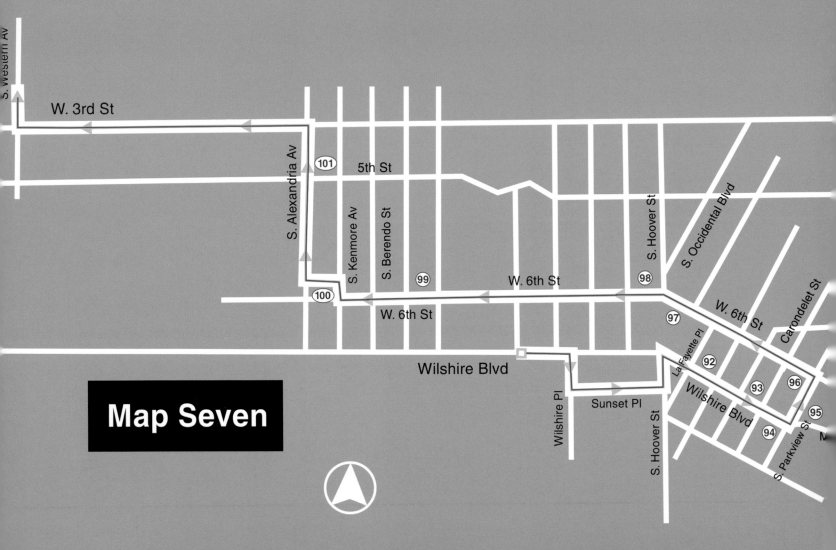

Map Seven

S. Western Av

W. 3rd St

S. Alexandria Av

(101) 5th St

S. Kenmore Av

S. Berendo St

(99)

(100)

W. 6th St

W. 6th St

(98)

S. Hoover St

S. Occidental Blvd

(97)

W. 6th St

Carondelet St

Wilshire Blvd

La Fayette Pl

(92)

(96)

(93)

(95)

Wilshire Pl

Sunset Pl

S. Hoover St

Wilshire Blvd

(94)

S. Parkview St

![arrow]

Left on Sunset Place; Left on Hoover Street; Right on Wilshire Blvd.

Lafayette Park is across the street as you continue down Wilshire Boulevard. This area is known as Wilshire Center. The skyscrapers of Downtown Los Angeles can be seen in front of you as you continue down Wilshire Boulevard.

92) The Bryson Apartments, coming up here on the left just past Lafayette Park Place, with the enormous Neo-Classical columns and statuesque lions gracing the entrance, were designed in 1912 by architects Frederick Noonan & Charles H. Kysor for Mr. Hugh Bryson. Now affordable housing, the restoration of the building was recognized with an award from the Los Angeles Conservancy in the late 1990s. This building is listed as Historic-Cultural Monument #653 by the City of Los Angeles. It is also listed on the National Register of Historic Places.

92) Bryson Apartments, 1912, Noonan & Kysor, 2701 WILSHIRE BLVD.

93) La Fonda Restaurant Building, on your left at the corner of Carondelet Street, was designed by Morgan, Walls & Clements in 1926 in the Spanish Colonial Revival style and is one of the oldest Mexican restaurants in Los Angeles. This building is listed as Historic-Cultural Monument #268 by the City of Los Angeles.

93) La Fonda Restaurant, 1926, Morgan, Walls & Clements, 2501 WILSHIRE BLVD.

94) Here on your right, at the southwest corner of Park View Street and Wilshire Boulevard, is the American Cement Corporation Building, designed circa 1961 by Daniel, Mann, Johnson & Mendenhall (DMJM). What makes this building unique is the innovative use of a concrete exoskeleton. Two hundred twenty-five X-shaped concrete modules have been placed in front of the windows, creating an exterior sculptural and textured form. This building was created as a showcase for the many uses of concrete and really highlights the sculptural quality of this utilitarian material. The exoskeleton also supports the building structurally and allows for the interior spaces to be open and free of support columns. Also notice the folded plate concrete roof on the base structure, further showing the flexibility of concrete. Once housing offices, the open spaces now lend themselves to their current use as large loft space apartments. This building is another excellent example of adaptive reuse. Views from the upper floors are of the Hollywood Hills, Downtown, and MacArthur Park across the street, named after General MacArthur.

94) American Cement Corporation Building, c. 1961, Daniel, Mann, Johnson & Mendenhall, 2404 WILSHIRE BLVD.

95) MacArthur Park

➡ Left on Park View

96) Here on your left is another massive building – the former Elks Lodge, now known as the Park Plaza Hotel, designed in 1925 by Aleck Curlett & Claud Beelman, who also designed The Talmadge and other structures seen earlier. Originally the lodge had a bowling alley, barber shop, swimming pool, and boasted a membership of 8,000 men. The grand scale of the building makes it stand out amongst the others. The large sculptures (quasi-caryatids) of idealized angel warriors (notice the wings) are a striking contrast to the sheer bulk of the box-like structure. Anthony Heinsbergen designed the interiors, which feature marble floors, a painted ceiling, and a chandelier of the Zodiac. On the exterior at the doorway are Corinthian columns and a clock with the head of an elk in the center. This building is listed as Historic-Cultural Monument #267 by the City of Los Angeles.

96) Elks Lodge (now Park Plaza Hotel), 1925, Aleck Curlett & Claud Beelman, 607 SOUTH PARK VIEW STREET

Left on 6th Street

97) Here on your left is the Felipe de Neve Branch Library at 2820 West 6th Street, designed by architect Austin Whittlesey in 1929 in a brick version of the Spanish Mediterranean style. The vertical bands of windows are each punctuated at the top by a white marble cross and surrounded by decorative brickwork in a diamond pattern. The arched entrance with a dark wood door is enhanced by the polychrome terra cotta tile and cast decoration. A terra cotta pipe roof tops it all. This building is listed as Historic-Cultural Monument #452 by the City of Los Angeles.

97) Felipe de Neve Branch Library, 1929, Austin Whittlesey, 2820 WEST 6TH STREET

98) Here on your right, at the northwest corner of Occidental Boulevard, is the massive First Congregational Church of Los Angeles, designed by Allison & Allison, Austin Whittlesey in 1932 in the Gothic style. These architects also designed the Wilshire United Methodist Church seen earlier. This building is listed as Historic-Cultural Monument #706 by the City of Los Angeles.

98) First Congregational Church of Los Angeles, 1930-32, Allison & Allison, Austin Whittlesey 540 SOUTH COMMONWEALTH AVE.

99) Coming up quickly on your right, on the northeast corner of Berendo Street, is the Founder's Church of Religious Science, designed in 1957 by Paul Williams, whose work you saw earlier. The Modern, circular church is enclosed by a wall of blocks that feature the Maltese cross formation. The legend is that the founder of the church suggested that Williams design the church in a round shape so "the devil couldn't hide in the corners," thus the round shape. This is an example of one of the few churches designed by Williams. This building is listed as Historic-Cultural Monument # 727 by the City of Los Angeles.

99) Founder's Church of Religious Science, 1957, Paul Williams, 3281 WEST 6TH STREET

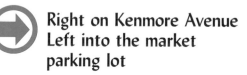

Right on Kenmore Avenue
Left into the market parking lot

100) Next, between Kenmore Avenue and Alexandria Avenue on 6th Street, is the Chapman Park Market & Studio, designed in the Spanish Colonial Revival style by Morgan, Walls & Clements in 1929 and restored in 1988 by Levin & Associates. The building is elaborately decorated with cast stone shield shapes, scrolling, and foliage all set upon a scored surface made to look like stone blocks. A wrought iron decorative pattern creates a border above the storefronts. A significant feature of this market was the inclusion of an interior motor courtyard. It was beginning to be recognized that more people were driving their own cars to shop and the merchants wanted to provide a place for their customers to park.

Across the street is an accompanying building originally built as artists' studios, now housing several photographers' studios. Notice the cast stone images of shields, victorious wreaths, and idealized warrior figures with helmets. This decoration was meant to refer to the Spanish Colonization of Mexico and California. The restoration of these structures has helped to revitalize the area. These buildings are listed as Historic-Cultural Monuments #386 (market) and #280 (studio) by the City of Los Angeles.

100) Chapman Park Market & Studio Building, 1929, Morgan, Walls & Clements, Restored 1988, Levin & Associates, 3465 WEST 6TH STREET

 Go through motor courtyard; Right on Alexandria Avenue; Pass 5th Street

101) This house, here on your right, is a beautiful example of a combination of Victorian and Craftsman architectural styles. It was designed in 1912 and built by contractor R.S. Gardner for Jay M. Decker. This house is similar to the houses seen earlier on Wilton Place with half-timber on the surface, exposed truncated rafter tails, and diamond pane windows. The front door is a typical Craftsman style large, wood door. This is one of the last remaining single-family homes in the area. It is very likely that there would have been more, but over the years have been replaced by apartment buildings.

101) Decker House, 1912, R.S. Gardner, 426 SOUTH ALEXANDRIA AVE.

Left on 3rd Street; Right on Western Avenue back to KFC.

Selected Bibliography

Gebhard, David and Harriette Von Breton. *Los Angeles in The Thirties: 1931-1941*, Second Edition, Revised and Enlarged. Los Angeles: Hennessey & Ingalls, Inc., 1989.

Gebhard, David and Robert Winter. *Los Angeles: An Architectural Guide*. Layton, Utah: Gibbs Smith Publisher, 1994.

Gleye, Paul. *The Architecture of Los Angeles*. Los Angeles: Rosebud Books-The Knapp Press, 1981.

Herr, Jeffrey ed. *Landmark L.A.: Historic-Cultural Monuments of Los Angeles*. City of Los Angeles Cultural Affairs Department, Santa Monica, California: Angel City Press, 2002.

Kaplan, Sam Hall. *LA Lost and Found: An Architectural History of Los Angeles*. New York: Crown Publishers, 1987.

McGrew, Patrick and Robert Julian. *Landmarks of Los Angeles*. New York: Harry N. Abrams Publishers, 1994.

Pitt, Dale and Leonard Pitt. *Los Angeles A to Z: An Encyclopedia of the City and County*. Berkeley and Los Angeles: University of California Press, 1997.

Steele, James. *Los Angeles Architecture: The Contemporary Condition*. London, England: Phaidon Press, Ltd., 1993.

Index of Architects